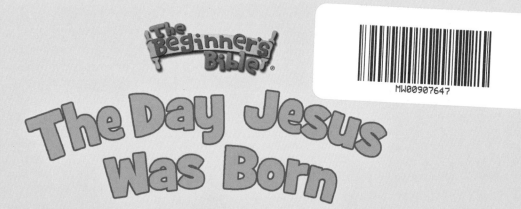

The Day Jesus Was Born

ZONDERKIDZ

The Beginner's Bible® The Day Jesus Was Born

Copyright © 2012 by Zondervan
Illustrations © 2012 by Zondervan

Requests for information should be addressed to:

Zonderkidz, 5300 Paterson Ave SE, Grand Rapids, Michigan 49530

ISBN 978-0-310-72517-6 (softcover)

Written By: Crystal Bowman
Editor: Mary Hassinger
Cover & Interior Design: Cindy Davis

Printed in China

ZONDERVAN.com/
AUTHORTRACKER
follow your favorite authors

12 13 14 15 16 17 18 /LPC/ 12 11 10 9 8 7 6 5 4 3 2 1

When Jesus was born, it was a very special night. Some shepherds were outside watching their sheep. Suddenly, an angel appeared before them. The sky became bright. The shepherds were afraid.

The angel said, "Don't be afraid. I bring you good news of great joy. A Savior has been born in the town of Bethlehem. He is Christ the Lord! You will find the baby wrapped in cloths and lying in a manger."

Then more angels appeared in the sky. They praised God, singing, "Glory to God on high! And on earth, peace and goodwill to all people."

The shepherds said, "Let's hurry to Bethlehem to see this wonderful thing the Lord has told us about." And there they found the baby, who was lying in the manger just like the angel had said.

The shepherds went out and told everyone about Jesus and all the things the angel had told them.

Then the shepherds returned to their sheep. They praised God for everything that had happened.

Joseph and Mary took baby Jesus to the temple in Jerusalem. A man named Simeon was there. He held Jesus in his arms. "I have seen the Savior," he said. Joseph and Mary were amazed at his words. Then Simeon blessed them.

A prophetess named Anna was also at the temple. When Anna saw Jesus, she thanked God and told everyone, "This is Jesus, our Savior and King."

On the night Jesus was born, some wise men saw the bright star God had placed in the sky. They knew it meant that a king had been born.

So the wise men followed the star and traveled a long way. They finally came to Jerusalem.

The wise men asked King Herod, "Where is the newborn King? We have come to worship him." King Herod was upset. He did not want someone else to be the king. Herod found out that Jesus had been born in Bethlehem. He told the wise men, "Go to Bethlehem. When you find him, tell me where he is so I can worship him too."

The wise men followed the star to Bethlehem where they found Jesus. They bowed down and worshipped him. They gave him gifts of gold, frankincense, and myrrh.

When it was time for the wise men to go home, an angel in a dream told them to go home a different way. This made Herod very angry!

God also sent an angel to Joseph in a dream and said, "Take Mary and Jesus to Egypt. Stay there until I tell you to return." Joseph did what the angel told him to do, and they left that very night.

A few years later, after Herod died, God sent an angel to Joseph in a dream. "It is safe to go back home now," the angel said. So Joseph, Mary, and Jesus went to live in a town called Nazareth. Jesus grew up and was very wise.

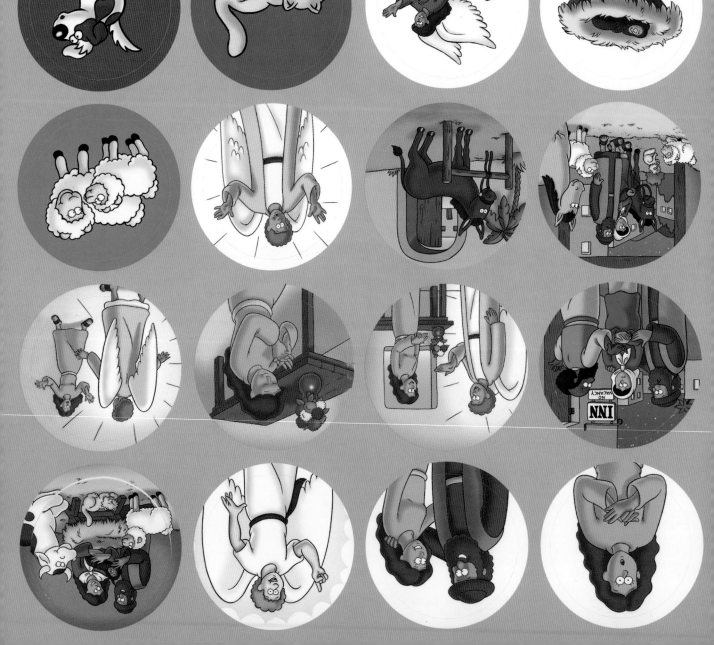

And that very night, something wonderful happened—the baby Jesus was born! Mary wrapped him in warm cloths and laid him in a manger.

The only place where they could stay was in a stable with the animals.

It was a long trip for Joseph and Mary. When they finally got to Bethlehem, they were very tired. Mary was soon going to have her baby. Joseph and Mary went to the inn, but all the rooms were full.

So Joseph and Mary traveled from Nazareth in Galilee to Bethlehem in Judea. Bethlehem was also known as the city of David.

While Mary was still pregnant, Caesar, the new leader of Rome, decided to count all the people under his rule. He ordered all the people to go to their homeland to register. Since Joseph's family was from the town of Bethlehem, that is where Joseph and Mary had to go.

When Joseph woke up, he did everything the angel of the Lord had told him to do. He loved Mary and promised to be her husband.

The angel said, "Joseph, you must take Mary to be your wife. The baby inside of her is from the Holy Spirit. You will name him Jesus because he will save his people from their sins."

When Joseph found out that Mary was going to have a baby, he wanted to do the right thing. He did not want to shame her in front of other people. So Joseph decided to break their engagement in secret. But the Lord sent an angel to Joseph in a dream.

Mary finally understood the angel's message. She said, "I am the Lord's servant. May this happen to me just as you have said." Then the angel left Mary's home.

The angel said to Mary, "The Holy Spirit will be with you. The power of the Most High will cover you. The baby inside of you will be holy. He will be called the Son of God. Nothing is impossible for God! Even your relative Elizabeth is going to have a son in her old age."

Mary said to the angel, "How can this be? I am not even married."

The angel said to Mary, "Don't be afraid. God is pleased with you. You are going to have a baby boy. You will name him Jesus. He will be called the Son of the Most High. He will be a King, and his kingdom will never end."

Mary was a little frightened because she had never seen an angel before.
She did not understand what Gabriel was telling her!

A young woman named Mary lived in Nazareth, a town in Galilee. She was going to marry a man named Joseph, who was from the family of David. One day, God sent the angel Gabriel to give Mary an important message. "Greetings!" said Gabriel. "The Lord has blessed you, and he is with you."

The Angel Brings Good News

ZONDERKIDZ

The Beginner's Bible® The Angel Brings Good News

Copyright © 2012 by Zondervan
Illustrations © 2012 by Zondervan

Requests for information should be addressed to:
Zonderkidz, 5300 Patterson Ave SE, Grand Rapids, Michigan 49530

ISBN 978-0-310-72517-6 (softcover)

Written by: Crystal Bowman
Editor: Mary Hassinger
Cover & Interior Design: Cindy Davis

Printed in China

ZONDERVAN.com/
AUTHORTRACKER
follow your favorite authors

12 13 14 15 16 17 18 /LPC/ 12 11 10 9 8 7 6 5 4 3 2 1